Habits for Success

Why You Should Start Your Own Business Today

By: Stephen Rawlings

TABLE OF CONTENTS

Stephen Rawlings

PUBLISHERS NOTES

Disclaimer

DEDICATION

This book is dedicated to those who yearn to have their own successful business.

CHAPTER 1- ENTREPRENEURSHIP- WHY THINK ABOUT IT?

Entrepreneurship can seem like a risky proposition. Why go in to business for yourself when that could mean that your own savings or your own winning idea might get trampled in the dust? There is no denying that starting your own business can be a challenge, and that challenge may, ultimately, fail.

So why think about it? Well, as the saying goes, you cannot win if you do not play! Being an entrepreneur means being in charge, it means the risk is yours, but so is the financial reward. First, a look at ways to mitigate risk, then this chapter will focus on the fun part of all your hard work, the perks that come with being the one in charge!

To be an entrepreneur you don't necessarily need to put a lot of your own money on the line. For example, consider a franchise. It is a great way to mitigate both the risk of your business venture failing and the loss of your own invested money. Most Franchise opportunities mean you will be selling customers something they already want. A particular sandwich made a particular way, for example. Your customers already want the sandwich, and now they can get it from you! Your clientele is almost guaranteed, and your risk, compared to the exclusive high end boutique you have dreamt of running, is much lower! Some franchise buy-ins can be as low as $5000!

But you can be your own boss in many ways that are low risk; the hard part is the time it takes to get to a point of profit. For example, the internet is rife with blogs of all types, and almost all of them have some sort of advertising along the sidebar, or pop-up advertising along the bottom of the screen, or "sponsored content" written by the advertisers themselves, meant to blend in with the fresh content of the author(s). But guess what? All of that is revenue! In fact, many popular blogs get so well known that they get offered book deals! But again, this takes time. You need to build your "brand", get noticed and then get advertisers. However, this is also something you can do on the side, while you hang on to that day job that offers benefits and a 401K. Very little risk here!

But maybe these things are not for you and you just want to jump in with both feet with your awesome yoga studio in a cute storefront in a trendy neighborhood. As well as classes, you will offer a smoothie bar and fitness wear. Sounds awesome! But even if this is your studio alone, if you do nothing else, get your business incorporated as an LLC. It is very affordable to do this, and an LLC, or Limited Liability Company, boils down to one very, very important detail: if your business fails and you cannot pay your debts, your debtors cannot seize any of your other assets.

In layman's terms, if the cute yoga clothes you bought with your company credit card do not sell, and no one comes to class, and all your savings are gone, well, you can wash your hands of the whole venture and move on. The credit card company can repossess the yoga clothes and the smoothie blenders, but they cannot try and seize your car or your home or your personal savings. So, if you go this route, be sure to protect yourself with the simple measure of LLC status.

So, you brave entrepreneur! Now you know some ways to mitigate the risk inherent in starting your own business. A discussion of some of the perks of being the boss is next!

Have you ever had an awful boss? The power-tripping kind who has no clue how to do the job you're doing? It is infuriating, right? You could run circles around him or her! As an entrepreneur, you will never have to put up with that again! And you can run your own business as you see fit! Fairly, equitably, and above all, profitably!

Consider entrepreneurship because you can set your own hours. Sure, getting started might mean a lot of late nights, but get some success, a few employees, and leave at three to go to your kid's soccer game if you want. Granted, you might be back at five, or put in hours later once you have had a family dinner together and the child is asleep, but hey, no one was giving you a hard time about it. No one was docking your pay or telling you to talk to Human Resources to record your early absence and take the hours from your vacation time.

Which leads to another great perk of being your own boss; sure, you have worked hard all your life, but when it is your own business, you work even harder. You work even harder not just because it might be your money on the line, but because you want to work harder for yourself and your financial success. Instead of working because you have to fulfill a duty or a manager is "cracking the whip", now your hard work is for you!

And you know what happens when you can come in late to the meeting (since, hey, you are the boss and they cannot start without you)? And what happens when you can take the opportunity to catch that soccer game or have a long lunch? These little pleasures lower your stress levels!

Having the guts to become an entrepreneur might be stressful at first - getting funding, choosing your path via a franchise or your own storefront or financing your million dollar idea, but all that risk and hard work offers big rewards. Controlling the purse strings means guiding your profits, and calling all the shots means setting your own schedule and enjoying a less rigid, more fluid life.

Consider entrepreneurship because it is time for you to be the one in control!

CHAPTER 2- THE ADVANTAGES OF ENTREPRENEURSHIP

There are so many reasons why entrepreneurship is such a big draw for so many people. There are plenty of reasons why the possibility of owning a business is so alluring to some of us. It is about creativity, excitement, and so much more.

Excitement

There are some people who pursue entrepreneurship because it offers so much room for adventure. If you love to compete, there is plenty of fun to be had in the arena of entrepreneurial work. Building a business from scratch requires the drive to be competitive on a constant basis. When you finally see your finished product and the success it brings to you, you will feel completely amazed at the business you have created. This newfound excitement is incredibly invigorating for anybody who has been waiting for the perfect opportunity.

Creativity

It feels great to offer something that nobody else has seen before, a product that will possibly significantly benefit them in their lives somehow. This is truly a career that gives you the opportunity to put all your motivation to good use. You can brainstorm unique ideas for your product or service, in addition to creative marketing strategies. This is completely up to you. Nobody can stunt the growth of your business by telling you that you are not allowed to make specific changes.

Independence

So many people have an independent streak that encourages them to strive for the top without the need for an authority figure. The desire to be self-sufficient is entirely reasonable, even admirable. In the business world, this translates to independence. You have the full potential to create the business that you have been envisioning from the very beginning with no interference. You can create new products, change the services you offer or even change specific policies without addressing anybody else first.

Flexibility

You will find that working for yourself guarantees some level of flexibility. Nobody can force you to work certain hours. If you have an important family function, you can attend with no worries of losing your job. You can go on vacation whenever you want so long as you had made the necessary preparations. You are also allowed to create your own plan and adjust it accordingly. You might find that there are better ways of marketing your business after some experience. If you were answering to a boss, you would not be able to call the shots.

Potential to Make Money

Possessing the ability to make all the financial decisions for a company comes with more financial opportunity. These days, so many people feel that they are not being given the money they deserve for all their hard work. If you are the boss, you have the ability to determine how much money you deserve for a hard day's work. It is your decision as to how much money you get paid. You can say goodbye to the feeling of being short-changed. There are no limits on salary when you are the one writing the checks. In addition to having the ability to make money, you also have the ability to spend it as you see fit. You choose the way your company is funded.

Do What You Love

You will reach new heights of self-fulfillment when you are finally doing a job that you cannot live without. You are passionate about something; reach toward it. The more you actually work toward a career that you adore, the more you will learn to love the life you are living.

Create Balance

Some people are so caught up in work that they are unable to lead the personal life they dream of. Unfortunately, it is easy to become a workaholic. Becoming an entrepreneur can help you establish a firm boundary between work life and personal life. Of course, you must also be careful that you are not allowing work to take over your life too.

Job Security

You can have complete control of the future of your company when you are the boss. You can allow it to move in the direction you have chosen. If you make smart decisions, you can continue to move toward success. You have a job as long as you continue to make one for yourself.

Receive Recognition

If you are somebody who is tired of the boss always getting credit for your hard work, entrepreneurship might be a great choice. As the boss, you are the one receiving the recognition for all your work. People will learn that you have built the company from the ground up and become instantly impressed with the way you have handled all this responsibility.

Communicate Your Way

Some companies are not good at dealing with customers; this is just a fact that the business world must contend with. It is likely that you have even had to deal with poor customer service in the past. You can use your business to create solid customer service by setting your own policies. It is entirely up to you.

Establish a Company Culture

As the boss, you are the person setting the atmosphere for the company. If you create a positive workspace, the rest of your employees will follow suit. You need to establish a strong presence within the company, creating an environment that you actually want to work in. Nobody wants to go to work in an environment that they hate. You can establish a positive culture for your company by making choices that are welcoming rather than alienating.

Create a Cause

If you are an entrepreneur who wants to establish a local business, you may be doing more for your community than you can imagine. A new business can bring new revenue to the city and jobs to people who need them. You are also bringing new choices to consumers.

Every choice in life has a list of pros and cons to accompany it. You must weigh the good and bad elements of each item on the list to find out whether becoming an entrepreneur is something you are interested in.

CHAPTER 3- THE BENEFITS OF SETTING YOUR OWN WORK SCHEDULE

Ever wonder what it would be like to be able to set your own work schedule, instead of having to deal with the one you have been given? You actually can when you are your own boss and are self-employed. If you work for a company, they may even be able to give you the option to set your own schedule. Some companies only need a certain number of employees during certain time periods and this is where they are able to give the employee more freedom to choose what times they want to work.

There are several options available for you when you are your own boss and it comes to picking a schedule to work. This is for those that are self-employed. Self-employed individuals are going to have full control of when they will work or when they will take a day off. They have to be consistent in order to get the income they want to receive. The more they work, the more money they should make.

Self-employed individuals don't have to worry about vacation time off or having sick time. When they don't feel well, they can just relax and have the day off or work through it. It is completely up to them. They don't have to worry about getting fired for missing too many days. This is perfect for families that love to travel as well. They don't have to schedule the days off and hope that they get it. They can just schedule their vacation where they see fit.

Many individuals like to work for themselves because it works better for their family. This is ideal for both men and women. If the individual has children, they don't have to worry about missing games or school events. They can work around their child's schedule and have more family time. Even when the children are really young, those that are self-employed can work from home and take care of their young. This helps ensure they are not out the expenses for daycare services. On the days that they are unable to stay at home because of their type of job, they can just hire a babysitter or take the children to daycare on those days. This will reduce their daycare expenses compared to the normal five days per week schedule.

For those that are not self-employed, some companies will even give them the choice in choosing their own schedule. This would depend on the times they have available. They may have a list of what time slots or preset schedules they have available. The employee would then choose from that schedule and take what is available. They won't get to actually make up the schedule completely on their own. This does give them a better idea and they can choose if they want to work the early shift or a late one.

This is perfect for those that are morning people and for those who like to sleep in.

This type of scheduling system has been seen more when the company is open for 24 hours day, 7 days a week. Larger corporations, such as call centers, are able to have these types of options available for their employees. Some like to work during the day for they might have children at school. Others may need to work nights because of their life style. Everyone's situation is different and that is why it's important for them to have an opportunity to choose their schedule when possible.

Having a set schedule is going to help others better plan what they need to do each week. They will be able to have a better idea of who may be watching their kids and on what days. They will also be able to see when they can plan appointments for doctors or other needs. Many individuals like to work Monday through Friday and have the weekends off, whereas others like to have a day or two off during the week. The ones that like a day off during the week may have to go to the doctor more often. They don't have to worry about wasting their vacation or sick pay time to schedule these types of appointments.

Many companies will also give their staff an opportunity to work four, ten hour days instead of the usual five, eight hour days. The schedule can be a rotating schedule, meaning that their days off will change consistently. They will work so many days and be off so many days. This will keep their off days different. The employee will still know how to figure what days off they will have in order to plan their days off accordingly. Some of the companies that have the four, ten hour days will have set days. Meaning that the days off the employee will receive will be on the same days every week. The employee may be given the option of what days off they would like to have, if the company has the option available.

Stephen Rawlings

Getting to pick your own schedule if a huge benefit when it comes to working and there are several types of jobs that just tell you what you are going to work on a week or two in advance. It's hard to really plan anything in the future with these types of schedules. A set schedule, no matter if you are self-employed or not, is so much easier to work with. When trying to choose a job, if not self-employed, be sure to ask what their scheduling is like. This way you can determine if it is going to work with your life style and what you have going on, on a daily basis.

If you have never found the perfect job with the schedule you prefer may be wise to look into self-employment. There are corporations that need individuals to help sell their products or services but allow you to be in control. Some may even just start a business of their own so they can be in full control of all the money made.

CHAPTER 4- STARTING A BUSINESS- GETTING TO UNLEASH CREATIVITY

Starting a business is a long-term goal many people have at the front of their to-do lists. The idea of not having to work for employers and having freedom to make decisions on your own has apparently become appealing. But any great business or company starts out at the bottom. And it is in these initial months that challenges are most prevalent and daunting. In fact, failure during this stage can come as swift as how the idea came to light. Surviving until the end is, however, possible with the right mindset, sufficient resources, and limitless willpower.

Cultivate a Creative Mindset

Nowadays, ideas are scarce in any market or field you decide to stick your capital into. Every industry you look at will have hundreds of competitors who are more established than you are. Even the process of getting your brand name out to your target audience will prove to be an obstacle. Having a creative approach will allow you to offer something fresh and interesting to potential consumers. New ideas for products or services commands better prices and greater demand over time. This will catapult your business to the top of its respective market niche.

Planning All the Details

Having a great idea is insufficient to achieving something. You must also successfully enact it. This is where planning becomes important. Planning all major and minor details of your business is paramount. Plan both the offense and defense aspects of your business, such as cash flow, supply management, advertising, employee base, and so forth. Arming yourself with a plan avoids any pitfalls and loopholes and allows you to respond effectively to unforeseeable crises that come your way.

Determine your goals and objectives. Every entrepreneur has his/her personal reasons for starting a business. Is it because you love the idea of working in pajamas? Is your family involved in some kind of business and you plan on continuing it? Are your goals more of a long-term than short-term? Knowing your goals lays a concrete foundation on what your plan should be like and what ideas you stick with.

Know Your Budget

Your plan may encapsulate the budget details, but it is probably more appropriate to give it its own space due to the magnitude of its importance. Before identifying what equipment, supplies, and labor force you need or want, you must know how much capital you have and can comfortably spend. A $100,000 to $250,000 capital is a good starting point for small businesses and start-ups. Meanwhile, larger companies may require much greater capital. You should also have reserved cash for emergency situations and unplanned expenditures.

Set Good Prices

Pricing is a key factor that drives product sales. If a product is reasonably priced and has good value, it takes only little advertising for it to get established. If prices are too expensive, even if it has value, you will not achieve optimal sales volume. When setting prices, you should not only account for the costs of making the product, it should also generate income for your business. After all, you do spend your personal time and effort in acquiring these products. When thinking of the best price, stick with simple parameters and methods. You do not need any complex chart software or accounting abilities.

Find More Capital

Every company is limited with one thing - capital. Until you start raking in sales and profits, you must keep expenses to a minimum. Look for investors who are interested in putting their money into your business. It could be your grandparents, friends, colleagues, or anyone you know. Every buck can help increase your cash flow thus ultimately increasing purchasing power. Of course, you must first impress prospecting investors. That means you have to convince them that investing in your company will offer a greater return on investment than other vehicles for the long run. How you do this is up to you. Make sure you polish your ideas, dress professionally, and speak professionally.

Reaching Your Consumers

How do you reach your consumer? Whether they are miles away from your business or even states away, advancements in advertising has enabled businesses to bypass geographical challenges. So, what form of advert is best suited for your business? It could be billboards, online ads, posters, flyers, pamphlets, etc. The type of advert you choose will adjust the expenses, reach, and efficiency so be sure to give each option a thorough check and study.

Patience Is Crucial

Start-ups and small businesses will find the progress bar to be a bit slow, which is only normal. You cannot expect to achieve peak business growth overnight or after a few months. It takes years for a new business to become a respectable contender in its given niche. If you have neither the resources nor the patience to see your business through this period of time, you should take a break, sit down, and rethink your plans.

Benefits of Starting a Business

Aside from having a hold of your own schedules, you are also able to avoid the typical office stressors, such as varying political opinions, drama, conflicts, and so on. You also get to spend more time with your family and friends instead of getting stuck in front of your office desk for 50+ hours a week. Of course, these very benefits can also become the reasons for a more difficult business venture. Make sure you balance your privileges and keep a focused mindset towards your goals.

Make sure you have the physical and mental strength to become a proficient business owner. Since all responsibilities and outcomes are on your shoulder, expect a lot of stressful and discouraging moments along the way. If you are able to keep a headstrong and positive outlook, you can definitely pull off a business of your own. Remember albeit that starting a business is only halfway the journey, you must then maintain it and consistently grow the business until it becomes successful enough that it rakes in regular profits and a solid consumer base.

CHAPTER 5- HAVING OPTIONS- ADVANTAGES OF SECOND CAREER

Having more than one career provides several benefits. Some individuals choose to work in two separate careers simultaneously while others work in one career for several years and then choose to work in another career that takes them in an entirely different path after they have retired from the first. Either way, more and more people are choosing to work in at least two distinctly separate careers.

The misconception that people must choose only one career field and work in that area exclusively throughout their lives is without merit. In fact, this train of thought often limits individuals who are talented in more than one realm to feeling like they are forced to choose one career path or the other. This is unfortunate because many times they could effectively work in more than one career field and accomplish great things. Moreover, there are several reasons why a person may want to choose to work in at least two separate fields.

Monetary

Money is one of the most important factors that many people take into consideration when deciding on a career path. Unfortunately, several people find themselves in a struggle between doing something they love and doing something that will pay the bills. You must ensure that you are making enough money to be self supporting but it is equally important that you find your life's passion in your work in order to be truly happy in your personal and professional life. Therefore, some individuals make the decision to work in two distinctly different career paths simultaneously so that they can pay the bills and pursue the things that they truly love. Still others pursue two separate career paths simply because it is an essential fact of life that they must do this in order to make enough money to cover their expenses.

Versatility

One of the most effective ways to truly be an asset in the workplace is to have versatility. It is an essential part of maintaining viability within the workforce in an economy where even the most secure jobs are being cut. At times it seems as though there is no job security left in any field. Working in more than one career field helps to ensure that you have the versatility that is needed to keep working even when some of your coworkers are not as fortunate.

Work Ethic

Having a good work ethic is essential in order to remain successful and to make enough money to do the things that are truly important in life. Working in multiple career fields is one of the best ways to teach a good work ethic and ensure that you always remain interested in the work you are doing. This is especially true for anyone who has a tendency to get bored with the same routine easily because working in two different career fields at the same time gives them an opportunity to change the routine on a regular basis.

Self-Reliance

It is essential to be self-reliant. It has never been more important to be able to rely on oneself than it is today. The only certainty in life is that there will not always be someone waiting for another person to fall so they can pick them up and dust them off. Many times it is essential that a person do this for themselves. Working in multiple career fields can teach the self-reliance that is necessary in order to successfully do this.

Security

Working in more than one career field gives you a sense of security because you have income from more than one location. This is vitally important because if something should happen to one job there is still income from the other. While a person in this situation may not be able to experience the same standard of living that he or she is accustomed to, it is much better to have a portion of the overall income intact rather than having it dry up completely.

Sense of Accomplishment

Working in multiple career fields provides a sense of accomplishment because it helps people realize that they are talented enough to do two distinctly different things at the same time. It is unfortunate that many individuals choose one passion over another because they feel that they must settle on only one path. For example, many individuals who have the ability to analyze data or form plans also have a great deal of artistic ability, but feel that they must leave one or the other behind. Those who simultaneously pursue both sides of their abilities often have a greater sense of accomplishment.

Stephen Rawlings
Self-Satisfaction

Having the ability to work in more than one career path often leads to self-satisfaction because the individual in question is no longer torn between choosing one thing over the other. This is something that has the potential to tear an individual apart if they feel that they must choose one career over the other because they feel that they are in fact leaving a part of themselves behind. Making the conscious decision to pursue all of their interests with passion and dedication leads to a great deal of self-satisfaction and a life of contentment.

There are many reasons that working in more than one career field is beneficial. Whether the reasons are out of necessity or out of a conscientious effort born out of desire, the results are often the same. People are likely to find that they are happier in their work and that they are also more financially secure. In addition, working in multiple career fields allows individuals to explore their own desires and talents to the fullest extent possible.

Many times this leads individuals to working in fields where they previously thought they had no chance of finding the ideal job. Openly exploring talents and pursuing jobs that an individual feels passionate about is important because it leads to a greater feeling of fulfillment while the person is working. The fact that additional financial security is provided both while actively working and after retirement is yet another reason to pursue more than one career path in life.

CHAPTER 6- STARTING A BUSINESS- REKINDLING THAT PASSION

It's a proven fact: people who start their own business are often happier than those who work for others. But people who own their own business also work longer hours than those who depend upon others to sign their paychecks. And while calling all the shots and being your own boss can be exhilarating, it can also be exhausting. Never ending demands on your time combined with the stress associated with a "make it or break it" scenario can make even the most dedicated entrepreneur question what he or she is doing.

Burnout is a common problem among entrepreneurs. The stress can lead to decreased job performance, strained relationships, and health problems. Thankfully there are ways to combat burnout and rediscover the joys that led you to starting your own business in the first place.

Schedule Time for Yourself

Entrepreneurs work hard. They have to. The bills don't get paid unless they do.

But that drive can quickly drain the passion out of what is supposed to be the perfect job. As Stephen King pointed out in "The Shining," "All work and no play make Jack a dull boy." It's true. Constant attention can turn anything into a burden.

Allowing business to take up constant residence physically, mentally, and emotionally is a recipe for burnout. Instead, take time out for yourself. Find ways to unwind and focus on other aspects of your life. Spend an evening out with friends. Have a date night. Make a rule that you will not answer your business phone after a designated time, and stick to it. Give yourself the gift of time

Stephen Rawlings

away from work, like a scheduled workout or an appointment for a manicure. Taking time for yourself actually gives you more energy that allows you to take better care of your business.

Delegate

Entrepreneurs, particularly those just starting out, often find themselves running the entire business by themselves. Everything from the bookkeeping and bill paying to changing the toilet paper falls on their shoulders. A lot of the time those little hassles cause the biggest headaches.

If this sounds like you, find a way to stop the madness. Though the thought of single-handedly running a business is noble, it's often not practical. Take a close look at the tasks that need done. Cross any off the list that aren't essential to the business. Of the tasks left, identify the jobs that you do not enjoy. Figure out a way to delegate those tasks to someone else. If you can afford it, hire someone to do those jobs. If you can't afford to have anyone else on payroll, get creative. Find a student who needs job experience, trade goods and services with someone else, or enlist the help of a willing family member. While it may seem easier to just do it on your own, that kind of thinking can lead to incurable burnout.

Find a Mentor

Some entrepreneurial ventures are lonely. It can be easy to wallow in despair when you feel like you are the only one who ever went through a particular challenge. However, that is rarely the case. Although you may be in business by yourself, you don't have to be alone. Find someone in a similar field who is willing to help you learn the ropes. People are more willing than you may think. Business relationships often reap rewards for both parties. Look to people you admire, or find other professionals through social media. If all else fails, look into hiring a business coach who can help you figure out how to rekindle your passion. These relationships don't have to fill large blocks of time to be effective. Meeting for coffee every now and then or corresponding through emails is often enough.

Break Out Of a Rut

Think about how you felt when you began your business. You were probably excited and brimming with new ideas. Now look at yourself now. What's different? As people fall into a routine, it's normal to lose some of the creative focus and drive that propelled them forward in the first place. Change can be good, so evaluate your own situation. Are you bored? No longer challenged? Lacking new ideas? Find ways to shake it up. Rearrange your work space. Take a class to learn something new. Start a blog. Launch a new product. Re-imagine your marketing. Some people are able to rediscover their passion simply by reconnecting with their creativity.

Figure Out What's Missing

Though starting your own business may be a dream come true, it may not meet all the needs you have as an individual. In fact, the energy you spend on your business may come at the expense of another area of your life. Figure out what's missing and fix it.

Maybe it's helping others through volunteer work. Maybe it's family time or important relationships. Whatever it is, identifying it may help you feel whole.

Believe In Yourself

A rocky patch is enough to suck the passion out of even the most enthusiastic person. Maybe a client was unnecessarily harsh. Or the business's performance slumped for a short time. Perhaps you got bad feedback or an unkind review. These kinds of events can shake anyone's confidence enough for them to question whether they are really the right person for the job.

The truth is that these kinds of things will happen. And they will happen more than once. The key is to learn from them and move on. Maybe you did mess up an important order. Figure out how it can be handled differently next time. Perhaps the negative feedback resulted from a subpar performance. Pledge to do better.

Failure allows a person to learn and grow in ways that are more meaningful than lessons found in success. Remember the reasons you chose to start your business and focus on why you are the ideal person to meet your customers' needs. You may be able to fake competence, but few people can fake the enthusiasm that helps customers believe in you and your product.

Chapter 7- Starting a Business- Opportunities for Philanthropy

When you start a business there are many opportunities to serve your community and the world around us. Understandably, if you have recently started a business, most of your funds will be allocated to start-up costs and advertisements. Philanthropy need not be an expensive endeavor and ultimately can help grow your business as you show a willingness to be part of your community.

One great opportunity is to be a location for a food drive. Many of the organizations will provide a box to your business to collect donations and will then list your business location on their website as a site for which those interested can drop off shelf-stable goods. Participating in a food drive will only cost your business a bit of floor space for the few weeks the food drive lasts.

The benefits of participating will go on, though as those in the community learn the name of your business and visit it throughout the food drive. Usually food drives will be advertised throughout the community through flyers and advertisements on local TV and radio stations. You can also visit your local radio station's website to find out about any food drives they sponsor. Usually, the radio station will have contact information for businesses interested in participating.

Another opportunity is to participate in a fund raiser for a charitable organization. One such organization is Relay for Life, which funds research to find a cure for cancer. With Relay for Life and similar organizations, there is a small registration fee for each team – for businesses the teams would be made of up employees. The team pledges to raise a certain amount of money and then each team member is responsible for gathering his or her share of the goal amount. Then, on the day of the Relay, the goal is to have at least one member from each team on the track from 6pm – 6am.

The community is encouraged to come out and support the teams and there are many activities that go on during the Relay. Your business would only have to set up a booth, which is a great way to get involved with the community while advertising your business at the same time. You could provide product samples at your booth and display banners with your company name. You could also give away inexpensive items such as pens or pencils personalized with your business's name and phone number. The more the people in your community see you involved, the more they will recognize your brand and want to do business with you when they need your products or services.

Another great way to give back to your community is to become involved with your local schools. Many public schools will ask businesses to sponsor them, which can get costly. Your business can help in other ways, though. When the school has an event, such as a fall carnival, ask if you and your employees can volunteer to help. You may also offer to donate items to give away for prizes.

Many businesses will use this opportunity to give away coupons or small gift cards. There may also be other opportunities to contribute, such as buying a small add in a program for a school play or giving the school a discount if you offer services they need.

Encouraging your employees to contribute to organizations they care about is also a way support your community even when you are just starting your business. You might think about offering a more flexible schedule to allow them to volunteer, for example. Many businesses offer to match employee's donations to charitable organizations up to a certain amount per pay period. If you are just starting your business, make sure you set an amount that is financially feasible for your business as it starts and also as it grows and you hire more employees.

Although it is always great to contribute to your local community, you may also want to participate in larger organizations. Many of the world-wide charities will allow a business to contribute at different levels of sponsorship. They will usually also provide a business with a decal to display. This will encourage your customers to contribute and also show them that you are a business that cares about our world. You can also participate with organizations that pack food boxes (the food and boxes are supplied) or shoe boxes filled with necessities for those less fortunate around the world. You may consider inviting your customers to your business to help pack the boxes, you may be surprised by how much business you do during the time they are there.

Many businesses also donate a portion of their profits to organizations they care about. If your customers care about the same organizations, they will be more likely to buy from you, as long as you keep your prices competitive. Don't be afraid to display this information at your store front or on your website. Telling your customers about the things you care about may also encourage them to donate to the same charities.

Although not usually financially doable for businesses just starting out, if you would like to set up a program to offer grants to your employees to further their education, make that a goal from the start. You may find that in a few years you are able to start offering these grants as a benefit to your employees. Many businesses that offer these types of incentives to their employees find that their employee retention rate is much higher than that of businesses that do not. This is because an employee will feel very loyal to a business that cares about helping them achieve their personal goals.

As your business becomes established, you may find that you are getting more requests to contribute than you can handle. Setting a budget the best way to make sure that you know exactly how much, if any, you can give to each request. Once you make a budget, you can then decide if you would like to donate a larger amount to a few organizations or smaller amounts to several organizations. No matter which you choose, you will show by example that you are a business that cares about improving your community and our world.

ABOUT THE AUTHOR

Stephen Rawlings knows that everyone has to make their own decisions when it comes to their career. His decision to pursue entrepreneurship was the best decision he has ever made in his life. Encouragement to do so came to him from many directions. But initially he's the one that held himself back by making excuses for why he just couldn't get started. His biggest regret is that he didn't start sooner. The wasted time lost will not come back.

However, Stephen refuses to allow himself to dwell on that anymore and have freed himself to make a success of his own business. He believes that we can hold ourselves back or we can allow ourselves to dive in and see just how wonderful being an entrepreneur really is. Even if your business fails, get up and dust yourself off and then try going for another one. You will have more experience and make better decisions. He knows because it happened to him. But things are going great now. He doesn't look back. This can be the same outcome for you.